Know Your True Self

The information provided in this guide is designed to provide helpful information on the subjects discussed. This guide is not meant to be used, nor should it be used, to diagnose or treat any medical or mental health conditions. For diagnosis or treatment of any medical or mental health conditions, please contact your health care provider or a licensed physician.

ISBN: 978-1-7346691-4-5   paperback
        978-1-7346691-5-2   hardback
        978-1-7346691-3-8   ebook

Cover: Lance Buckley / lancebuckley.com

Interior: Julia Roberts / prismamedia.co

PTNL

Published by PTNL

www.ptnl.com

Know Your True Self

THE FORMULA TO RAISE HUMAN CONSCIOUSNESS

James Petrossi

PTNL

To Humanity,
*May we evolve and prosper
in the spirit of harmony.*

Acknowledgements

To the many forces that have helped in the creation of *Know Your True Self.*

Universal Intelligence

Thank you for the human experience, self-awareness, and all of the natural wonders on planet earth and beyond.

Robert Petrossi

Your relentless quest for knowledge into the true self inspired, shaped, and guided the development of *Know Your True Self*; for this, I am eternally grateful.

Wise Humans

A special thanks to all of the scientists, psychologists, philosophers, and spiritual teachers whose contributions to humanity are reflected in *Know Your True Self.*

James and Emily Vance

You continue to be beacons of light in my life. Thank you for your spiritual contributions to this endeavor and the love you have shared over the years.

Fairfield University

The education I received at Fairfield helped shape my perspective on consciousness. Thanks to all of the faculty and staff in the psychology and communications departments.

Patricia and Samantha Petrossi

Thank you for believing in this message and for all of your support throughout the development process.

"Knowing yourself is the beginning of all wisdom."

- Aristotle

Table of Contents

Preface

It took 200,000 years for humanity to reach one billion people, but after that, it only took 200 more years for the population to skyrocket to almost eight billion people. While innovations such as farming, electric engines, vaccines, computers, and the Internet have helped propel the human species forward, exploding population growth, non-stop innovation and relentless change do have unpleasant side effects.

It's alarming to think humanity spends trillions of dollars on health and wellness, but physical and mental illness rates continue to rise. Technology has us more connected than ever before but is a root cause of anxiety and depression. Heart disease, diabetes, and cancer are at epidemic levels. Relationships have become increasingly fractured, many feel unfulfilled at work, and we're recovering from a global pandemic. Now what?

How can humanity overcome these evolutionary challenges and others? That starts with each of us identifying with and acting through our true selves. Unfortunately, knowledge of the true self is not typically taught in formal education. Some of us go to school for 12 years or more and receive little or no education into the true self. Then as adults, we tend to focus on skill-based training for career development and personal growth.

What could be more important for humans than knowing their true selves? Could this educational shortfall be the primary reason for humanity's suffering and dysfunction? Teaching humans to be human®, to evolve and prosper in the spirit of harmony, was why I chose to create *Know Your True Self*.

This guide was developed from decades of research, learning, and personal experience shared between me and my father, Robert Petrossi. It uniquely integrates, distills, and synthesizes essential knowledge from countless sources of inspiration into a simple, proven formula designed to help humans help themselves.

Robert began as a seventh-grade educator, found his way into sales, and then formed a global training company in the 1990s that integrated life-skills education into Fortune 500 business practices. After retiring due to illness in 2008, he has been on a quest for knowledge of true self while serving as a lifelong mentor to me.

Inspired by working alongside Robert from a young age, I went on to study Psychology and Organizational Communications at Fairfield University. Since then, I've spent the past 20 years developing human-centric marketing, sales, and coaching strategies for leading global and emerging growth organizations.

When I almost lost my father to cancer in 2018, I left my career as Senior Vice President of Creative Strategy and Development with a renowned entertainment and cultural marketing agency to found PTNL. With the vision of creating a more consciously connected world, I began working full time on creating *Know Your True Self*.

Soon you will discover that the layout of this guide is not typical of most books. Its design helps focus the attention of readers whose brains have been rewired from repetitive internet use. The majority of the pages begin with a headline question. Then you'll find answers in a series of connecting ideas displayed in visually engaging formats that aid in the learning and retention process.

After learning key concepts, self-reflections throughout this guide will help you look inward on the journey to identifying with and acting through your true self. Readers have the option of just thinking through the self-reflection questions raised on the page or having a pen and paper available if they desire to take more detailed notes.

Since the content in *Know Your True Self* puts readers first, you will not hear any personal stories about my journey, but I can assure you that developing this guide has transformed my life in many ways and continues to do so every day.

Learning and practicing the principles within it has helped me overcome ignorance, denial, trauma, fear, relationship challenges, health scares, worry, and addiction. Professionally, the knowledge contained in this guide has been instrumental in my growth as a business leader and success in leading high-performance work teams.

Now that the opportunity to make a positive change is in your hands, I hope this guide becomes a trusted resource on the journey to know your true self.

A first edition of Know Your True Self was published in 2020 with a slightly different subtitle; this newly revised second edition has been redesigned and contains over 80 new content pages, including self-reflections, based on valuable feedback from readers.

Introduction

What is the purpose of this true self discovery guide?

To help raise human consciousness.

Why know your true self?

The innovations responsible for humanity's growth have severed the connection with our true selves, which is the root cause of today's challenges.

Who is this guide designed for?

The principles in *Know Your True Self* work equally well for all humans who have the desire to create more peace, joy, and contentment in life.

What is the underlying premise?

Solving humanity's key evolutionary challenges begins with humans learning to identify with and act through their true selves.

When humans practice actions to raise their own level of consciousness, they help to raise the consciousness of humanity.

What are some of today's key challenges?

HEALTH

Obesity

Depression

Heart disease

Cancer

Pandemics

RELATIONSHIPS

Divison

Social injustice

Split families

Aging parents

Time spent online

WORK

Constant change

Little job security

Long work hours

Artificial Intelligence

ADDICTION

Prescription drugs

Illegal drugs

Food

Alcohol

Social media

ENVIRONMENT

Overpopulation

Sustainability

Climate change

Pollution

Food chains

The evolutionary challenges created from rapid population growth and non-stop innovation have left many humans struggling to find peace in everyday life.

How can humanity overcome these challenges?

Teaching humans to be human®.

The simple truth.

The ability to identify one's true self is not instinctive for most humans and must be taught.

The shocking reality.

We have instruction guides for almost everything from furniture assembly to computer programs, but we are never formally educated on the true self.

The self-education challenge.

Humans have more information, knowledge, and insight into the true self than ever before, but they often fail to see the big picture of how it all fits together so they can flourish in life on earth.

Know Your True Self provides humans with a simple, proven formula to raise their level of consciousness.

What is the formula to know your true self?

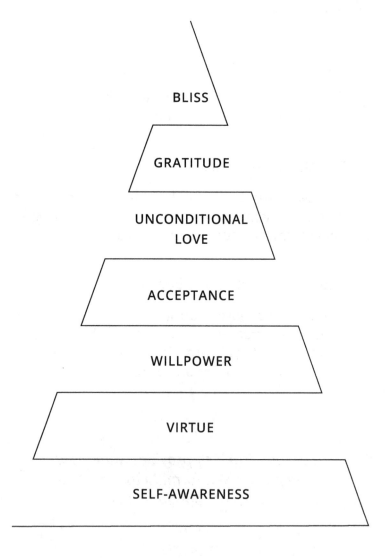

BLISS

GRATITUDE

UNCONDITIONAL
LOVE

ACCEPTANCE

WILLPOWER

VIRTUE

SELF-AWARENESS

What are the benefits of knowing your true self?

Limitless in potential.

Truth.

Since the dawn of time, humans have pursued the truth about the nature of their existence. Who am I?

Power.

Humans that identify with their true self have the power to navigate life experiences with peace and joy.

Enlightenment.

Humans become enlightened when they practice actions to stay centered in and act through their true selves.

Life is chaotic and unpredictable; the formula to know your true self helps to bring order to the chaos inherent in human life.

What might surprise you in the learning process?

The convergence of human knowledge.

Diverse knowledge, theories, and beliefs all point to the same true self.

The integration of human knowledge will be the catalyst for the next evolution of education into the true self.

How will you get the most out of this guide?

Active participation.

Learn.
Become educated on the content, concepts, and insights provided on each page.

Reflect.
Take time to self-reflect on how the concepts apply to your own life experiences.

Practice.
Make a daily effort to practice actions designed to raise your level of consciousness.

Become your own teacher and advocate.

On the journey to knowing your true self, you have to look inward and become your own teacher and advocate. You have to learn to help yourself.

Change comes from within and requires a commitment to personal growth. There are no shortcuts to discovering your true self.

Enjoy the journey.

THE FORMULA TO KNOW YOUR TRUE SELF

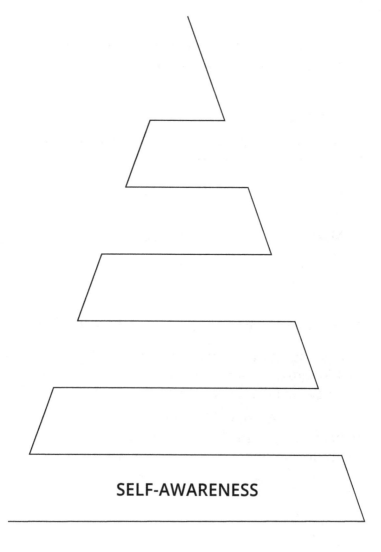

SELF-AWARENESS

What is unique about human consciousness?

Self-awareness.

Humans have the unique ability to observe one's thoughts, emotions, sensations, and behaviors.

Children become self-aware around 18 months of age, but practicing self-awareness requires work throughout life's journey.

Self-awareness is the basis for knowing the true self.

What is a common false belief about human consciousness?

That understanding consciousness is intuitive.

Consciousness is not commonly taught in formal education and is seldom understood by the masses.

Without knowledge of consciousness, it is difficult for humans to identify with and act through their true selves.

THE ILLUSION OF CONSCIOUSNESS	DIVIDED CONSCIOUSNESS

Many humans falsely believe that the thoughts generated from their mind are their true self.	Smartphones, social media, and technology all hijack and divide human consciousness.

Most humans are not conscious of their own consciousness.

How can humans learn about self-awareness?

Keep an open mind.

Understanding the nature of consciousness requires an open mind to look beyond one's current view of reality.

Seek the truth.

 Discover the origin, evolution, and key principles of universal consciousness.

 Know how the human mind operates both consciously and unconsciously.

 Be aware of the many self-awareness roadblocks and how to navigate them.

Understanding consciousness provides humans with the knowledge to better understand themselves, others, and the universe's underlying laws.

Self-awareness

THE EVOLUTION OF CONSCIOUSNESS

What is the source of consciousness?

Universal Intelligence.

Universal Intelligence expressed itself 13.8 billion years ago through the Big Bang when light exploded out of nothingness and darkness.

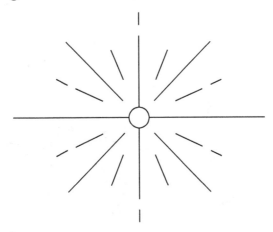

This massive explosion of energy eventually cooled, forming galaxies, stars, planets, and life forms.

Humans are living relics of the Big Bang.

When searching for truth, the answers lie not in looking down at our phones but in looking up to the sky, and questioning the source of creation and our human connection to it.

What is a misconception about the universe?

Separateness vs. wholeness.

Humans perceive less than 5% of the universe, which gives us a limited view of reality.

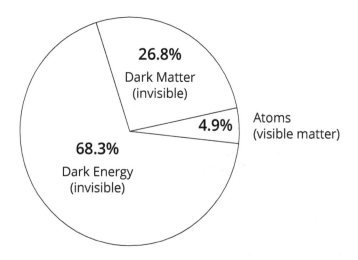

26.8%
Dark Matter
(invisible)

4.9%
Atoms
(visible matter)

68.3%
Dark Energy
(invisible)

Human Perception.

There are separate objects in space that may or may not be related to each other somehow.

Reality.

Everything visible and invisible to humans is part of and connected to one Universal Intelligence.

15

What is mysterious about the atoms in humans?

Now you see it... now you don't.

Wave-particle duality is an atoms' ability to behave like particles or waves, meaning there is a visible and invisible nature to human existence.

ATOM PARTICLE	ATOM WAVE
●	
Visible and occupies space like the form of the human body.	Invisible and ripples through space like human consciousness.

"Spooky" science.

Quantum entanglement states that two particles can be linked, so what happens to one particle will instantly affect the other particle, even if that other particle is light-years away.

Human relationships are entangled; just thinking about someone close to you can initiate a phone call from them.

How are humans entangled with all life on Earth?

The universal energy field.

The atoms that makeup humans are the same as the atoms that make up air, water, plants, fish, and animals.

Humans are entangled with each other, with other living creatures, and with the environment through a universal energy field.

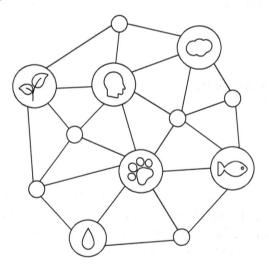

When humans help to create balance in nature, they also help to create balance within themselves.

Self-Reflection

Connectedness.

Humans are not separate from each other; they are all connected through the same field of energy.

Do I ponder the nature of my existence? How?

What is my connection with Universal Intelligence?

Do I perceive myself as separate from others? Why?

Who are the people I'm most entangled with?

Does their energy affect mine and vice versa? How?

In what ways do I connect with and protect nature?

What is the physics of Universal Intelligence?

The Law of Conservation.

Everything in the universe, both visible and invisible to humans, is part of a closed system of energy that can be thought of as a Universal Intelligence or connected consciousness.

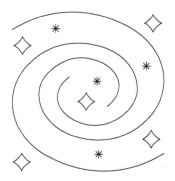

Energy cannot be destroyed.

The total amount of energy in the universe always remains the same, but the way the energy is distributed throughout the energy field constantly fluctuates.

The energy that gives consciousness to life is not bound by physical form. Upon death consciousness continues to exist, but in what fashion remains a mystery.

What distributes energy throughout the Universe?

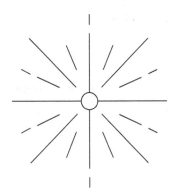

Unknowable Light.

Light is a source of creation.

Light never changes.

Light is absolute.

Light is formless.

Light is infinite.

Light is eternal.

Humans never actually see light.

The human perception of darkness does not mean light is absent.

The light perceived by humans is known only through the energy it releases and the limited frequencies of the senses.

While light exists in the visible world, its invisible nature permeates throughout all of life and creation.

How have humans interpreted the mystery of light?

As a source of life, love, and creation.

Primitive humans.

Primitive humans instinctively recognized the divine nature of light by worshiping the sun for its life-sustaining capabilities.

Spiritual teachers.

Throughout history, spiritual teachers, prophets, and mystics have often referred to light as a Universal Intelligence or God.

Popular culture.

Light is a common theme used in many songs to describe feelings of unconditional love and bliss.

"You are my sunshine."

"You light up my life."

"Turn on your love light."

> *"For the rest of my life, I want to reflect on what light is."*
> -Albert Einstein

Is the human experience physical or spiritual in nature?

Spiritual.

Humans often identify with their mortal physical self because it can be touched and seen, but it is the invisible nature of humanity where the true self resides.

Spirituality is the belief in a formless, eternal energy force or light within each human connected to Universal Intelligence.

How do humans learn about spirituality?

Through the teachings of great prophets, mystics, and spiritual teachers.

Religious and spiritual groups.

Scientific research.

Observing nature.

Personal experience.

The human spirit, or inner light, is the source of energy that is human consciousness.

Self-Reflection

Spirituality.

The human spirit is the connection point to Universal Intelligence and the source of human consciousness.

Do I identify with my physical or spiritual self? Why?

What role does spirituality play in my life? Why?

How do I connect with or nurture my spiritual self?

What spiritual groups do I belong to? Why?

Do I believe people have soulmates? How come?

How do I share my inner light with the world?

What is the link between light and consciousness?

The present moment.

Light and consciousness exist in a state where there is no past or future; there is only now.

LIGHT

CONSCIOUSNESS

The theory of relativity states that, if traveling at the speed of light, time would stand still in the present moment.

Consciousness only exists in the present moment because the past and the future are illusions of the human mind.

We often get lost in our minds, obsessed with a past that we cannot change and worrying about a future that does not exist, yet the true self only exists in the present moment.

Self-awareness

THE HUMAN MIND

How have the functions of the human brain evolved?

REPTILIAN BRAIN	MAMMALIAN BRAIN	THINKING BRAIN
500 million years old.	*50 million years old.*	*2.5 million years old.*
MAIN FUNCTIONS	**MAIN FUNCTIONS**	**MAIN FUNCTIONS**
Survival and reproduction.	Social interactions / emotions.	Higher-order thinking skills.
Unconscious control of bodily functions.	Identifies friends and potential enemies.	Language, creativity, visions, and dreams.

The human brain is like a big antenna. The senses allow for messages from the visible world to be received and decoded.

How do humans perceive the visible world?

Indirectly.

Everything that humans experience through their senses has been reconstructed from sensory data in the brain, creating the mind's contents.

Example:

1. Light reflects from an object.

2. Reflected light forms an image of the object on the retina of the eye.

3. The signal then travels down the optic nerve to the visual cortex of the brain.

4. Visual cortex processing in the brain transforms signals into shapes, patterns, colors, sensations, and movements.

5. The brain then integrates this sensory information into a reconstruction of the external world, which appears as an image in consciousness.

Every life experience is stored in the human mind, even though we cannot readily recall most life experiences.

How is the brain like a computer?

Input = Output.

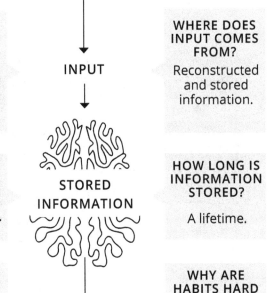

HUMAN LIFE EXPERIENCES

INPUT

Data from the five senses and unconscious memories.

WHERE DOES INPUT COMES FROM?

Reconstructed and stored information.

INPUT

STORAGE

Information gets stored in neuron chains.

STORED INFORMATION

HOW LONG IS INFORMATION STORED?

A lifetime.

OUTPUT

Thoughts, feelings, behaviors, and actions.

OUTPUT

WHY ARE HABITS HARD TO BREAK?

Old programs (neuron chains) remain in brain storage.

RESPONSES TO LIFE EXPERIENCES

How are the human brain and the mind different?

HUMAN BRAIN CHARACTERISTICS	HUMAN MIND CHARACTERISTICS

An organ in the body.	No weight.
About 3.3 pounds.	No shape.
Shaped like a wrinkly walnut.	No cells.
86 billion nerve cells.	No blood vessels.
Can be touched.	Cannot be touched.

_____ _____

Healthy human brains are similar in structure.	Human minds are uniquely different.

_____

The human mind operates both consciously and unconsciously.

"Biology gives you a brain. Life turns it into a mind."
-Jeffrey Eugenides

What caused humans to become aware of their consciousness?

The development of language.

After the "thinking brain" or cerebral cortex developed in humans, a new language capability emerged and changed the course of human consciousness.

PRIMITIVE HUMANS

Before language, humans, like all living creatures, lived moment to moment through an intuitive consciousness.

MODERN HUMANS

Humans began thinking about past and future events with language, creating a separation from the present moment.

The epic milestone of language frayed the connection of humans living solely in the present moment.

How did humanity benefit from language?

Strengthened tribal connections.

Communication.

Humans developed language in the forms of symbols and words to connect all tribal members' collective consciousness.

Survival.

Language helped improve survival skills, which eventually led humans to exploit the environment and fueled human population growth.

Knowledge.

The sharing of information empowered humans to create knowledge databases, inspiring new forms of creativity and innovation.

Language empowers humans to share thoughts, ideas, and cultural perspectives to learn from one another.

What evolutionary challenge did language create?

Two human minds.

Humans began to use language internally and started to have discussions with themselves.

THE GIFT	THE CHALLENGE
Humans became, for the first time, aware of their own existence.	Humans lost the intuitive connection to universal consciousness.

Identifying and knowing the true self has been an ongoing challenge for humankind.

What are the characteristics of the two human minds?

THE UNCONSCIOUS MIND	THE CONSCIOUS MIND

It keeps humans safe.	The gift of choice.
Responsible for survival and reproduction instincts.	Responsible for decision-making and creativity.
Regulates the human body.	Controls impulses from the unconscious mind.
Acts on impulses.	Includes the sensations, perceptions, and feelings experienced in the moment.
Creates an identity based on all of its life experiences.	

Many humans falsely believe they control their actions, but research indicates that about 95 percent of human behaviors are unconscious.

When does the unconscious mind develop in humans?

Early childhood experiences.

Everything learned in the first six years of a child's life is stored as truth because a child's mind is impressionable and highly imaginative.

Childhood experiences unconsciously impact adult human behavior, both positively and negatively.

Trauma example.

Ten million children are exposed to domestic violence every year, making them significantly more likely to be abused as adults or to harm others.

The good news.

Unpleasant childhood experiences can be neutralized through self-awareness, professional counseling, and acting through the true self.

All humans experience trauma in life; not all humans learn to address their trauma.

Self-Reflection

Traumas.

Like a scratched record, the unconscious mind will periodically replay traumatic life experiences.

What traumatic experiences have I endured?

Do any past traumas impact my life today? How?

Do I hold on to these traumatic events? Why?

How have they impacted my perception of life?

How would it feel to move past my traumas?

What support can I seek out to help find peace?

What shapes the content of the unconscious mind?

Personal and tribal associations.

WHAT HUMANS IDENTIFY WITH	WHO HUMANS IDENTIFY WITH
Birthplace	Family
Education	Nationality
Life experiences	Religion
Work	Race
Activities	Culture
Brands	Politics
Possessions	Group affiliations

The content of the unconscious mind varies from human to human because everyone's life experiences are different.

How does the unconscious mind cause distress?

Nonstop comparisons.

The unconscious mind compares and judges what humans experience in the present moment with its archives of past life experiences and knowledge.

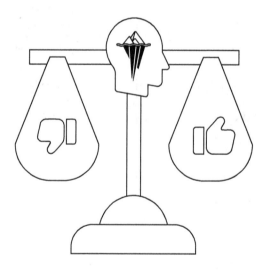

Since every human's life experiences are different, the unconscious mind is in a perpetual state of comparing, liking, and disliking.

Self-Reflection

Filtered lenses.

We all see the world through filtered lenses and make comparisons based on our own life experiences.

How did my upbringing impact my sense of self?

How have life experiences helped to shape me?

How have the groups I belong to shaped my beliefs?

Do I compare my life to the life of others? Why?

Do I judge people I don't even know? How come?

How can I compare less and appreciate more?

What example helps to explain human consciousness?

A movie projected onto a screen.

Human consciousness is like a screen where both present moment and memories from the past are displayed.

THE UNCONSCIOUS MIND (THE PROJECTOR)	THE CONSCIOUS MIND (THE SCREEN)
Like a projector, the unconscious mind projects images and thoughts from past life experiences.	Like a screen, the conscious mind receives input from the unconscious mind for observation.
Images and thoughts surface when there is an association/connection between a new and past life experience.	The conscious mind can observe both the present moment's reality and thoughts that arise from the unconscious mind.

Observation is the true power of self-awareness.

Why does the unconscious mind project memories?

To aid in decision-making and survival.

The contents of the unconscious mind are responsible for our protection and evolution as a species.

DECISION-MAKING	SURVIVAL
The unconscious mind is brilliant at connecting past experiences to create new ways of thinking.	The unconscious mind is vigilant in alerting humans to perceived dangers for its survival.
Association/connections with memories fuel creativity, helping humans make prudent decisions.	Association/connections with memories can also create many false, fear-based realities.
The genius of creativity lies in how the mind uses past experiences to solve new problems.	Humans have up to 60,000 thoughts daily, and approximately 80% of them are negative.

How can humans learn to identify perceived versus real threats?

Observation and reflection.

The human default mechanism sees the threat first, even if the perceived threat is not real.

These misrepresentations are called "false beliefs."

Examples of false beliefs:

PERCEIVED THREAT	REAL THREAT
Mistaking a rope for a snake.	Mistaking a snake for a rope.

THERE IS NO HARM.	THERE IS HARM.

Today's humans are overwhelmed with perceived threats generated by the news, advertising, and social media.

Self-Reflection

False Beliefs.

The newsfeed focuses on creating false beliefs because fear and worry drive clicks and views.

How often do I tune into the newsfeed? Why?

What are my most trusted sources for information?

Do they promote fear and worry? How?

Do they promote peace and joy? How?

When can I disconnect from the newsfeed?

How can I connect with the good in humanity?

Why must humans learn to train their unconscious mind?

To raise their level of consciousness.

The unconscious mind behaves like a wild dog.

If not trained, the unconscious mind will control its master through animalistic impulses.

Learn to train and live with the unconscious mind.

When trained, the unconscious mind obeys its master, and the true self reveals itself.

The unconscious mind is relentless in its desires.

Constant vigilance is required over the unconscious mind to overcome its impulses.

Self-awareness

ROADBLOCKS

Why is it difficult for humans to be self-aware?

Lack of education, technology, and impulses from the unconscious mind.

Self-awareness is a learned skill.

Learning to observe and direct one's consciousness is not intuitive but is obtainable for all of humanity through education and practice.

A divided human consciousness.

The Internet, smartphones, and social media hijack consciousness, distracting humans from living in the only actual reality, the present moment.

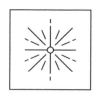

Self-awareness is easily blocked.

Self-awareness becomes blocked anytime humans identify with the desires and troubling thoughts that surface from their unconscious mind.

What are some of the self-awareness roadblocks?

APATHY FEAR ANGER JEALOUSY RESENTMENT

COMPLAINING IMPATIENCE

POOR NUTRITION SLEEP DEPRIVATION

Self Awareness

JUDGING NEWS

DENIAL ILLEGAL DRUGS

SOCIAL MEDIA PRESCRIPTION DRUGS

ALCOHOL ABUSE THE INTERNET HATE GUILT STRESS

Learning to navigate through the maze of self-awareness roadblocks is not intuitive for most humans.

What is the most common self-awareness roadblock?

Denial about the truth.

Denial is a natural survival instinct, but unconsciously living in it can cause humans a lifetime of pain.

How do humans express denial?

Simple denial.

When a human denies something unpleasant is happening.

Weather example: "I can't believe it's raining on my day off."

Minimization.

When a human admits something unpleasant is happening but denies how serious it is.

Obesity example: "I'm overweight, but my health is good."

Projection.

Projection occurs when a human blames others for an unpleasant event they caused.

Car accident example: "They were driving too slow, so it's their fault."

Denial is easy to see in other humans, but difficult to see in ourselves.

What are the consequences of living in denial?

Emotional and physical suffering.

Chronic stress.

The lack of self-awareness caused by denial makes it hard to release stress.

Internalized stress causes constant anxiety, which can lead to depression.

Illness and disease.

When the human body is continuously stressed, cells stop repairing and renewing themselves.

Living in denial for long periods can compromise the human energy system.

Seek support.

Overcoming denial takes courage.

Humans can ask family and friends to help identify the areas in their life that might need improvement.

Get professional help.

Self-Reflection

Denial.

Living in denial inhibits our ability to embrace reality, evolve as humans, and realize our full potential.

When have I been in denial about something?

How was I able to overcome my denial?

Is it possible I'm currently in denial about something?

What would my friends say I need to overcome?

What other self-awareness roadblocks do I face?

What's holding me back from addressing them?

How does social media block self-awareness?

Life comparisons and casting judgment.

Social media creates havoc on the unconscious mind through a never-ending feed of unfavorable comparisons to others' lives.

EXAMPLE

Tom checks his social feed and notices a friend's post from their birthday vacation to the islands.

Unconsciously Tom's mind makes a comparison with his recent birthday "staycation."

Tom's unconscious mind does not like the vacation comparison and concludes, "My life sucks."

Most humans are in denial about their addiction to social media and the havoc it plays on the unconscious mind.

What are the consequences of making comparisons?

Biological and emotional distress.

THE HUMAN BODY	THE HUMAN MIND
Jealousy triggers the human stress response.	Negative thoughts and emotions surface.
"My body feels tight and jittery for some reason."	"Nothing exciting or cool ever happens to me."

The consequences.

The unconscious mind perceives the social media comparison as a threat.

A single comparison can balloon to a false belief that everything in one's life is deficient.

Relationships with others suffer as the unconscious mind focuses on itself.

Social media is a brilliant innovation that connects humanity, but it should be used wisely with the knowledge of how the unconscious mind functions.

Self-Reflection

Social media.

Social media puts humans in a perpetual state of comparing, judging, liking, and disliking.

How has using social media benefited my life?

Has using social media caused me any pain? How?

Do I scroll endlessly for no reason at all? Why?

Do I need a phone in hand to feel connected? Why?

Have I lost the connection to my actual reality? How?

How would I benefit from a social media detox?

How does impatience block self-awareness?

Frustration and annoyance.

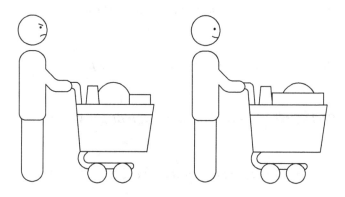

EXAMPLE:

You are in line at the grocery store.

One person is in front of you.

Ten people are in the other checkout line.

There is a price check in your line.

The other line empties while you are still waiting.

You become frustrated and annoyed.

Will getting upset over an event you can't control lead to suffering or peace?

Self-Reflection

Impatience

Impatience triggers the stress response, which hinders decision-making while blocking peace and joy.

When do I become impatient? Why?

How does being impatient affect my well-being?

Does my impatience affect others? How?

Why do I try to control what I cannot control?

When can I practice being more patient in life?

How would I benefit from being more patient?

How does anger block self-awareness?

Acts of rage and revenge.

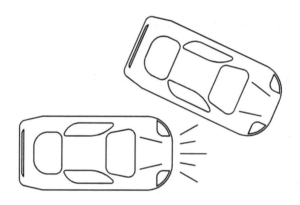

EXAMPLE:

A car cuts someone off in traffic; there is a split second in time that determines if the driver will respond unconsciously or consciously.

UNCONSCIOUS RESPONSE	CONSCIOUS RESPONSE
Honk the horn.	Reassess the environment.
Display anger.	Grateful for no accident.
Road rage.	Alert.
"I'm going after them!"	"Phew, that was close."

Self-Reflection

Anger.

Anger increases blood pressure, inhibits digestion, and weakens the immune system.

Do I get angry often? What are the usual causes?

When was the last time I was furious? Why?

How did I feel after the adrenaline wore off?

What did the anger do to my energy system?

How can I avoid situations that make me angry?

When can I replace my anger with tolerance?

How can humans make peace with their unconscious mind?

Rise above it; don't act through it.

Appreciate that the purpose of the unconscious mind is to regulate the body and keep humans safe.

Remember, the unconscious mind loses its power when the conscious mind observes it.

When humans embrace the reality of the present moment, the unconscious mind becomes quiet.

THE FORMULA TO KNOW YOUR TRUE SELF

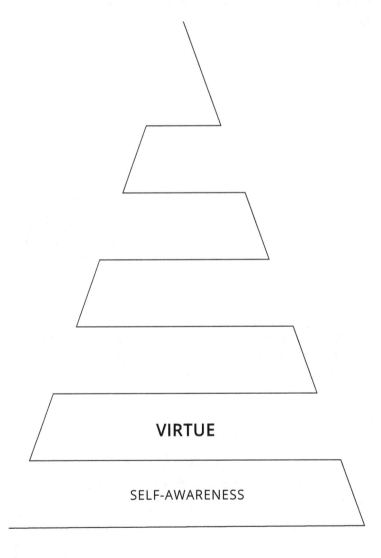

VIRTUE

SELF-AWARENESS

What does it mean to be virtuous?

To live one's life through the true self.

Self-aware humans begin the journey of realizing their potential when they create a conscious desire to help themselves, humanity, and the environment.

POTENTIAL IN NATURE   POTENTIAL IN HUMANS

The true nature of an acorn is destined to become the oak tree within it.

The true nature of a human is destined to become the spirit within it.

Living a virtuous life requires setting a personal goal not to harm oneself, others, and all living things.

What are the core human virtues?

Researched by Christopher Peterson and Martin Seligman.

WISDOM

To love learning and seek new wisdom.

COURAGE

To be brave, have integrity, and be persistent.

HUMANITY

To love, be kind, and help humanity.

JUSTICE

To be fair with others and a good citizen.

TEMPERANCE

To forgive, be humble, and have self-control.

TRANSCENDENCE

To have hope and humor, to be spiritual.

"Use your signature strengths and virtues in the service of something much larger than you are."
Martin E. P. Seligman

Why is it difficult for humans to live virtuous lives?

The desire to be virtuous is not instinctive for most humans.

THE MIND	THE TRUE SELF
Core virtues get blocked when the unconscious mind directs behavior.	Humans must practice self-awareness to act through their true selves.
Living life unconsciously can lead to addictions, vices, and unhealthy behaviors.	Self-aware humans find joy in developing, sharing, and fulfilling core virtues.

When humans put in the work to remove self-awareness roadblocks, they stay on the path of living a virtuous life.

Self-Reflection

Virtue.

The core virtues are all reflections of the true self that must be nurtured and developed throughout life.

Which of the core virtues comes naturally to me?

How do I currently practice or express them?

Are there virtues I could work on more? How?

What virtue is most difficult for me? Why?

What are the benefits of living a virtuous life?

Can I commit to living a virtuous life? Why?

How can humans connect to their true self?

Practice meditation.

Meditation quiets the unconscious mind's thoughts and helps humans connect with their true self and the vibrational frequency of Universal Intelligence.

Meditation brain science.

Meditation shrinks the amygdala, the region of the brain that triggers unconscious thought impulses.

Reduced stress.

Meditation also thickens the prefrontal cortex, the region associated with awareness, concentration, and decision-making.

Increased self-awareness.

Meditation brings the human energy system into balance and has countless applications for improving physical, mental, and spiritual well-being.

What is a simple meditation technique to practice?

The Relaxation Response.

Dr. Herbert Benson's research at Harvard University in the 1960s and 1970s is credited for the worldwide belief that meditation brings balance to the human body, mind, and spirit.

Three simple steps.

1. Sit in a comfortable position and close your eyes.

2. Relax all of the muscles in your body, beginning at your feet and progressing up to your face.

3. Breathe easily and naturally, and with each exhale of breath, recite the word "love" in your mind.

Meditation doesn't need to be complicated; start with five minutes once a day and progress to twenty minutes twice a day or more.

What are some helpful tips for practicing meditation?

Direct attention to your breathing.

Notice the inhale and the exhale of breath.

Slow down the rhythm of your breathing.

Feel your belly expanding and contracting.

Let go of the attachment to your senses.

Notice when the mind begins to wander.

Let go of any thoughts as they arise.

Come back to the rhythm of your breath.

Experience the weightlessness of self.

Feel your oneness with all.

KNOW YOUR TRUE SELF.

Self-Reflection

Meditation.

The practice of meditation comes in many forms, all designed to nourish the human spirit.

Do I accept the benefits of meditation? Why?

Do I currently practice meditation? How?

How does my energy system feel after I meditate?

When can I commit to meditating more?

How does meditating help to calm my mind?

When can I replace social media with meditation?

What state of consciousness can be achieved by meditating?

The transcendental state.

There is awareness during the transcendental state of consciousness, but there is no object of awareness.

MEDITATION	NATURE
During meditation, humans can transcend the thoughts that continuously surface from their unconscious minds.	Humans often experience the transcendental state when connecting with the vibrational frequency found in nature.

Reaching the transcendental state during meditation takes practice. Maintaining this state of consciousness while navigating through life's experiences is where the real opportunity lies.

What is the highest state of human consciousness?

The self-realized state.
Humans achieve the self-realized state when they are consistently aware of the present moment, embrace reality as it is, and use their talents to help humanity.

Non-attachment.

Through the power of observation, self-realized humans can separate illusion from reality by not identifying with the thoughts, fears, and desires generated by their unconscious minds.

Attainment.

Reaching the self-realized state is a gift available to all humans who look inward to seek the truth about life and its meaning.

Maintaining the self-realized state requires constant vigilance to stay centered in one's true self.

By not identifying with the unconscious mind, self-realized humans reflect the light of Universal Intelligence.

THE FORMULA TO KNOW YOUR TRUE SELF

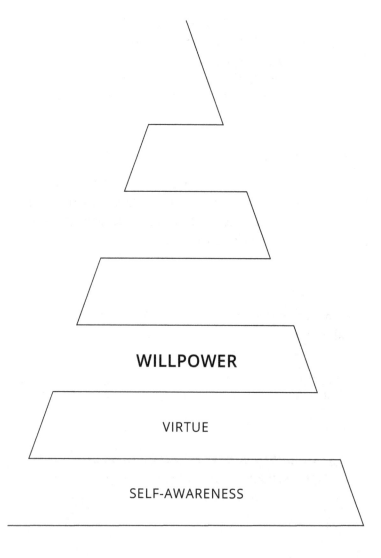

WILLPOWER

VIRTUE

SELF-AWARENESS

What is willpower?

A human energy source.

Willpower is the ability to resist impulses that arise from the unconscious mind through self-control.

THE UNCONSCIOUS MIND	THE CONSCIOUS MIND

Acts on impulses.	Controls impulses.
Seeks immediate gratification for rewards.	Delays gratification for long-term goals.

Exercising willpower over unhealthy desires is directly linked with increased well-being and happiness.

Unfortunately, innovations, technology, and advertising often weaken willpower by appealing to the unconscious mind's wants and desires.

Seeking rewards does not bring happiness; it brings only the promise of happiness.

Where does willpower get its energy from?

Glucose (brain fuel).

All humans have a limited supply of glucose, which fluctuates throughout the day.

Glucose levels are highest in the morning and begin to decline during the early afternoon.

Lack of sleep, stress, digital distractions, and making too many decisions all deplete glucose reserves.

How to keep glucose levels in balance?

Eat low glycemic foods like fruits, vegetables, nuts, fish, and lean meats.

Avoid making big decisions before meals, during the evening, or when tired.

Get ample sleep to restore glucose levels and the human energy system.

Dark chocolate stimulates an immediate increase in glucose levels and is recognized as a mind-boosting superfood.

What sabotages willpower?

The brain's reward center.

Dopamine creates a desire to seek rewards, which diminishes willpower and can lead to addictions.

The basic human survival needs such as food, shelter, sex, clothing, and protection are the catalysts for dopamine production.

SOME 21ST CENTURY DOPAMINE TRIGGERS

Processed foods	Housing options
Refined sugar	Destinations
Restaurants	Rewards programs
Delivery options	Online shopping
Online reviews	Flash sales
Social media	Streaming content
Friend requests	Prescription drugs
Followers	Security options
Likes	Insurance options
Dating apps	Subscriptions

Humanity is under siege from excess dopamine triggers, which is the root cause of chronic stress and addiction.

How can willpower help overcome dopamine triggers?

Habit formation.

Habits help to streamline repetitive brain processes, which conserves energy and prevents information overload.

The brain relies on routines.

The brain cannot function without habits, which is why nearly 95 percent of a human's daily actions are unconscious, repetitive habits.

Repetitive actions strengthen the connections between neurons in the brain, manifesting as either unhealthy or healthy habits.

New habits require new routines.

A change of environment and new routines are essential to replace unhealthy habits with healthy ones.

Replacing habits takes time; it can take between 21 to 90 days or longer for new habits to take root.

While unhealthy habits fade over time, the neuron chains associated with them never totally disappear.

What is the biology of creating new habits?

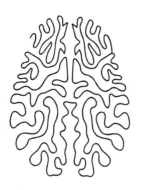

Brain plasticity.

The human brain is not hardwired; it is continuously reprogramming itself based on input from one's thoughts, actions, and life experiences.

Habit formation is determined by where a human focuses their attention for an extended period.

THE HUMAN REALITY	THE HIDDEN DANGER
Humans without physical brain damage have within them the power to:	Unconsciously rewiring the human brain for unhealthy habits leads to:
CONTROL THEIR DESTINY	ADDICTION AND SUFFERING

Brain plasticity allows humans to take an active role in identifing with and acting through their true human self.

How can humans strengthen their willpower?

Create new, healthy habits.

Practice self-awareness.

Observe the thoughts and impulses that surface from the unconscious mind before acting on them.

Keep brain chemistry in check.

Maintain adequate glucose levels in the brain and ignore dopamine triggers that weaken one's willpower.

Control your breathing.

Initiate the relaxation response or meditate to help overcome unhealthy desires and create balance.

Redirect consciousness

Waiting 10-15 minutes before taking action weakens the impulses generated by the unconscious mind.

Self-Reflection

Willpower.

Humans rely on willpower to overcome the relentless desires that arise from the unconscious mind.

How often do I act on impulses? Why?

How do I keep my glucose levels in check?

What desires do I overindulge in? How come?

What are some of the triggers for my desires?

What is the one unhealthy habit I want to change?

What new healthy habits will that change create?

What is needed to create new habits?

Change.

The brain and the unconscious mind will resist change, even if the desired change is positive.

Adapting to change can make humans feel lonely and disconnected as consciousness refocuses from past routines to new ones.

Fear and worry often surface as the unconscious mind focuses on the past and future, neglecting the present moment.

Tips for creating positive change.

Be persistent.

Don't feel guilty or give up after a setback.

Believe change is possible to form a new habit.

Remember, new habits require new routines (repetition).

Keep a support group informed of your progress.

Stay focused on the benefits of new habit creation.

Over time your new habit will require no effort.

Good habits naturally produce other good habits.

THE FORMULA TO KNOW YOUR TRUE SELF

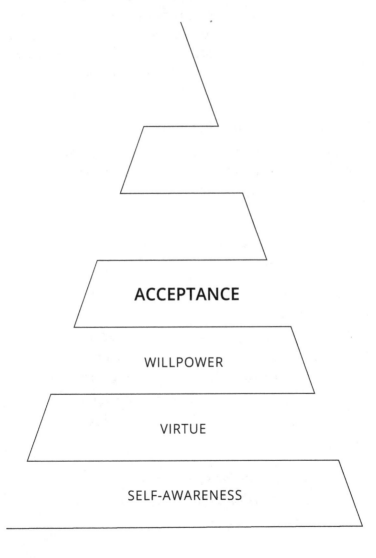

ACCEPTANCE

WILLPOWER

VIRTUE

SELF-AWARENESS

What is acceptance?

Embracing reality as it is.

Life is chaotic and unpredictable, so humans must learn to embrace the moment they are in because the past and future are merely illusions created by the unconscious mind.

How is acceptance learned?

When humans understand what they can and cannot control, they become equipped to navigate life's uncertainty through acceptance.

HUMANS CANNOT CONTROL	HUMANS CAN CONTROL
The past	Choice
The future	Goals
Life events	Attitude
Other humans	Kindness
The weather	Forgiveness
Aging	Gratitude
Death	Love

Humans suffer every time they try to control what is not in their control.

What does practicing acceptance mean?

It is what it is.

Practicing acceptance does not mean that navigating the change associated with unpleasant or unpredictable life experiences will be easy.

Practicing acceptance does mean a human embraces the underlying reality of the life experience by finding the opportunity within it.

What does living a life of acceptance look like for humans?

Going with the flow of life experiences.

ACCEPTANCE	NON-ACCEPTANCE
Humans believe life experiences are *neither* good nor bad.	Humans believe life experiences are *either* good or bad.

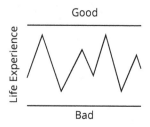

"It is what it is."	"This can't be happening."

"Don't seek to have events happen as you wish, but wish them to happen as they do happen, and all will be well with you."
- Epictetus

Self-Reflection

Acceptance.

Life is unpredictable, so to find peace in it, humans can embrace all moments without judgment.

When in life have I had to practice acceptance? Why?

What was at the root of my non-acceptance?

How was I able to move past it? How did that feel?

Is there currently something I'm not accepting? Why?

What is in my control? What is not of my power?

Is it possible to know what is good and what is bad?

What are the characteristics of accepting humans?

They are physically and emotionally calm.

TRAITS OF ACCEPTING HUMANS

Empathetic	Content
Compassionate	Grateful
Forgiving	Enthusiastic
Generous	Peaceful
Engaging	Helpful

Accepting humans live in the present moment, and it's a joy to be with them.

What are the characteristics of non-accepting humans?

They are physically and emotionally stressed.

TRAITS OF NON-ACCEPTING HUMANS

Complaining	Jealous
Blaming	Revengeful
Judgmental	Fearful
Resentful	Angry
Anxious	Impatient

Non-accepting humans live in the past and the future, and it's draining to be with them.

What is the typical path to acceptance?

Kübler-Ross grieving model.

This model applies to any catastrophic event, such as terminal illness, job loss, divorce, or financial setback.

STAGE 1 DENIAL	STAGE 2 ANGER	STAGE 3 BARGAINING
Humans block the current reality.	The reality of the situation sets in.	Try to manipulate the situation.
"This can't be happening."	"I can't handle this."	"If only I had done things differently."
They seek a false, preferable reality.	Emotions run high as fear surfaces.	Vulnerable and helpless feelings.

STAGE 4 DEPRESSION	STAGE 5 ACCEPTANCE
Not able to cope with the situation.	Embracing the new reality.
"I give up."	"It is what it is."
Period of isolation and distress.	Living through the true self.

It's common for humans to move between stages of grief in a nonlinear manner.

What is the danger in the grieving process?

Sometimes humans get stuck in it.

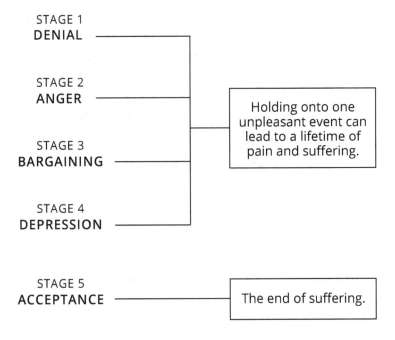

STAGE 1
DENIAL

STAGE 2
ANGER

STAGE 3
BARGAINING

Holding onto one unpleasant event can lead to a lifetime of pain and suffering.

STAGE 4
DEPRESSION

STAGE 5
ACCEPTANCE

The end of suffering.

"The most beautiful people we have known are those who have known defeat, known suffering, known struggle, known loss, and have found their way out of those depths."
- Elisabeth Kübler-Ross

Self-Reflection

Grieving.

Grieving is a natural process that humans go through. Learn to navigate it wisely to avoid getting stuck.

When have I had to cope with loss in the past?

What loss has been the most challenging for me?

How well did I navigate the stages of grieving?

How did it feel when I reached acceptance?

Am I currently grieving about anything? Why?

What is at the root of my nonacceptance?

How can humans weather unpleasant events?

Remember these four simple words.
"This, too, shall pass."

LIGHT	DARKNESS
Sometimes pleasant emotions surface that bring "light."	Sometimes unpleasant emotions surface that bring "darkness."
(such as peace and joy)	(such as fear and worry)

Finding Peace.

Peace comes from the truth that unpleasant events are transitory and will pass, just like the natural cycles of day and night.

"Character cannot be developed in ease and quiet. Only through the experience of trial and suffering can the soul be strengthened."
-Helen Keller

What is an example of practicing acceptance?

Company reorganization.

Job loss can feel like doom and gloom or be perceived as an opportunity to learn, grow, and evolve as a human.

NON-ACCEPTANCE	ACCEPTANCE
REACTION	**REACTION**
"I'll never be able to get another job!"	"If I have to find a new job, it will be a chance to grow personally and professionally."
FEELINGS	
Hopeless, sad, worried, anxious.	**FEELINGS**
	Calm, in control.
BEHAVIORS	
Self-pity, moping, and giving up.	**BEHAVIORS**
	Optimistic, confident.
IMPACT ON FAMILY AND FRIENDS	**IMPACT ON FAMILY AND FRIENDS**
Tension, despair.	Relieved, proud.
THE BOTTOM LINE	**THE BOTTOM LINE**
Stress and suffering.	Peace and contentment.

How can humans learn to accept other humans?

Celebrate diversity and practice inclusivity.

Humans are not separate from one another; we are all connected through the same universal energy field.

DIVERSITY	INCLUSIVITY
More unites humans than divides them, but the unconscious mind only focuses on what's different.	When humans embrace diversity, new ways of thinking emerge to help serve all of humanity.

The power of connectedness.

When humanity's diversity is woven together in the spirit of acceptance and unconditional love, the human species will realize its true potential.

Cultural differences are an illusion of the unconscious mind. The only true cultural association is humanity.

THE FORMULA TO KNOW YOUR TRUE SELF

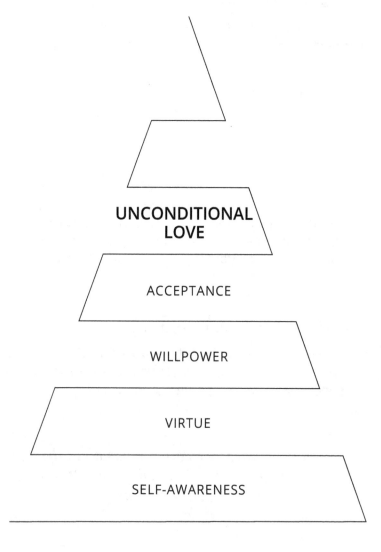

UNCONDITIONAL
LOVE

ACCEPTANCE

WILLPOWER

VIRTUE

SELF-AWARENESS

What is the **first step** to loving unconditionally?

Love one's self.

Self-love comes from the awareness of being one with Universal Intelligence and recognizing that the true self connects to the source of one's creation.

Self-love is practiced by caring for oneself. It requires nourishing the human energy system, forming meaningful relationships with others, and focusing on personal growth opportunities.

Reasons humans don't love themselves.

They compare themselves to others.

They hold on to mistakes made in the past.

They have fear and uncertainty about the future.

They feel pain from traumatic experiences.

They do not accept their unique traits.

Self-love should not be confused with self-obsession, narcissism, or arrogance.

Where is the vibration of unconditional love found?

The human heart.

The universal symbol of love, the human heart, starts beating before the brain forms, and its vibrational energy is essential for developing and sustaining life.

Vibrational energy and entrainment.

When two objects of like vibration are in proximity, the item with a weaker pulse will begin to match the stronger beat.

The heart has the strongest vibration in the human body and entrains all other cells with its beat frequency.

IN BALANCE	OUT OF BALANCE
	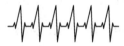
A calm, restful heart rate that entrains with the vibration of nature and Universal Intelligence.	A stressed, rapidly beating heart rate that entrains with the thoughts of the unconscious mind.

How do humans practice self-love?

Create balance.

MIND	BODY	SPIRIT
Live in the moment.	Eat healthy foods.	Relax and meditate.
Embrace reality as it is.	Set exercise goals.	Develop natural talents.
Be grateful for life.	Get ample sleep.	Connect with nature.

Accept one's self.

To practice self-love, humans must learn to love all the unique qualities and characteristics that make them special in the world.

Humans should not compare themselves to others. Making unfavorable comparisons is a root cause of anxiety and depression.

What is an indicator of self-love?

Self-talk.

Positive self-talk originates from the true self, while negative self-talk is a byproduct of the unconscious mind.

UNCONSCIOUS MIND	TRUE SELF
"I'm a loser."	"I'm a loving person."
"No one loves me."	"I deserve to be loved."
"I always screw up."	"It's okay to make mistakes."
"I'm worthless."	"I'm proud of my talents."
"I hate the way I look."	"I'm beautiful as I am."
"I'll never amount to anything."	"I'm grateful for the gift of life."

To attract loving people and have meaningful relationships, humans must first learn to love themselves.

How is self-love shared with others?

Friendships.

Humans are highly social, and forming meaningful friendships with others increases one's sense of belonging and purpose. It also improves self-confidence.

Helpful tips for nurturing friendships.

Make an effort to be genuinely interested in all people.

Remember people's names, say them frequently.

Listen and let other people talk about their interests.

See the world from the other person's point of view.

Give sincere compliments whenever possible.

Avoid arguments; when wrong, admit it.

Make people feel appreciated.

Don't criticize.

Smile.

Humans have relied on love, friendship, and meaningful social connections to survive as a species for over two million years.

How can humans strengthen relationships?

Spend more time with their inner circle.

It's not how many friends a human has that matters, but how they nurture the relationships that matter most to them.

When humans become addicted to social media, they often lose sight of their most meaningful social connections.

Self-Reflection

Self-love.

We seek to receive love from others, often neglecting that we must first learn to love ourselves.

What unique traits do I love about myself? Why?

How do I care for my mind, body, and spirit?

What areas of self-love can I improve? Why?

Do I need to forgive myself for anything? Why?

Do I reward myself for personal achievements?

How can loving myself help me to love others?

What is the **second step** to loving unconditionally?

Display empathy.

Empathy is the uniquely human ability to imagine other humans' thoughts, feelings, and emotions to foster meaningful connections.

When humans take time to display empathy through active listening, they can earn the trust of other humans by learning about their needs to determine how they can help.

Why empathy works?

Empathy helps humans connect intellectually by understanding another person's life experiences.

Empathy helps humans connect emotionally by sharing the feelings another person is experiencing.

> *Seeing the world from another human's point of view is the crucial link in human communication.*

What is the biology of empathy?

Mirror neurons.
Mirror neurons are specialized brain cells that track what other humans think, feel, and do.

Humans are hardwired for empathy.
When observing the behavior of others, the human brain simulates what they are watching.

PHYSICAL	BEHAVIORAL	EMOTIONAL
Humans mirror each other's body language.	Humans mirror other's behaviors and actions.	Humans mirror other's emotions and feelings.

Example: Someone yawns, and others who witness the act begin to yawn, too.	Example: If your friend wants a cup of coffee, you also want a cup of coffee.	Example: When a person cries while telling a heartfelt story, you also begin to cry.

How does empathy develop in children?

Facial mimicking with parents.

A positive, nourishing attachment with parents is vital for the social and mental development of children.

Infants imitating the facial expressions of their parents play a crucial role in the development of empathy.

POOR PARENTING	QUALITY PARENTING
The lack of parental bonding and learning facial mimicking inhibits a child's ability to distinguish between positive and negative emotions.	Children raised by loving parents display greater empathy, have better social skills, and are more skilled in managing their own emotions.

Unpredictable living environments, absent parents, and the lack of positive social exchanges with other humans often leads to crime and violent behavior.

101

How do humans effectively display empathy?

Focus attention on the feelings and emotions of others.

Listen.

Active listening is one of the best ways to help those in need to share their feelings and emotions.

Examples:

"Tell me more about how you are feeling."
"How did that experience make you feel?"

Confirm.

Paraphrasing what the other human said confirms your understanding of their feelings and emotions.

Examples:

"I can understand your dog's death is hard on you."
"It must have been tough being at the funeral."

Share.

Empathy's power comes from sharing the feelings and emotions of others.

Examples:

"I feel your pain."
"That breaks my heart, too."

Why is active listening so difficult for humans?

They think faster than others speak.

Humans process information four times faster than a person can speak, making it difficult to pay attention to what is being communicated to them.

Traits of good listeners.

Good listeners make an effort to listen. They talk less and ask follow-up questions to learn more.

AVOID CLOSED QUESTIONS	ASK OPEN-ENDED QUESTIONS
Closed questions elicit only a "yes" or "no" response and make humans feel pressured and defensive.	Open-ended questions help create a dialog, help to build trust, and ensure more time for listening.
EXAMPLE:	EXAMPLE:
Are you upset?	*How do you feel?*

Listening requires focus and concentration.

103

What happens when humans lack empathy?

Antisocial personality disorder.

Antisocial personality disorder occurs when the human brain's moral reasoning centers are underdeveloped or have become injured in humans.

SYMPTOMS	CAUSES
Not able to see right from wrong.	Genetic factors.
Persistent lying.	Lack of loving facial mirroring.
Arrogance.	Abuse or neglect.
Recklessness.	Unpredictable living environments.
Lack of remorse.	
Abusive relationships.	An unstable family life.

The hard truth.

Although there is no cure for genetic dispositions, better parental education, mentorship programs, and professional counseling in early childhood can reduce antisocial behavior.

Those that lack empathy require our compassion and forgiveness.

Self-Reflection

Empathy.

Empathy is a crucial link in the communication process that helps humans understand each others' feelings.

How often do I express empathy? When and why?

What can I learn by understanding others?

Who can I display more empathy to in life? Why?

What difficult challenges are they currently facing?

How can I listen better and ask more questions?

How does being empathetic to others help me?

What is the **third step** to loving unconditionally?

Have compassion for other humans.

Compassion is lessening the suffering of others through understanding, acceptance, and involvement.

THE GIFT TO HUMANITY	THE BENEFIT TO HUMANITY
Compassion sprouts from empathy and is the gift of clarity that we are all connected, and no one human is better or worse than another.	Compassion strengthens human connections, bridges cultural divides, and brings unconditional love into the world through human actions.

Compassion requires humans to engage in helping others navigate through life's challenges.

How can humans practice compassion?

Become educated.
Learn more about the cause of a person's suffering, such as poverty, depression, substance abuse, divorce, etc.

Be sensitive.
Refrain from telling someone who is suffering that everything is okay; this well-intentioned communication strategy makes the sufferer feel more isolated and alone.

Provide support.
Seek positive ways to help others by listening to their emotional needs while taking an active role in offering suggestions for professional help or counseling.

Show affection.
Hugging or holding someone's hand results in a lower heart rate and reduced stress, and even a simple smile can bring temporary relief from emotional pain.

Be patient.
Remember that suffering blocks hope, forgiveness, and self-awareness.

Healing takes time.

How do humans show compassion to others in need of help?

Acts of service.

Spiritual teachers, police, fire, rescue workers, healthcare professionals, teachers, and all service professionals dedicate their lives to helping others.

There are more than 1.5 million charitable organizations in the U.S. alone, and an estimated 25 percent of adults have volunteered their time for just causes.

Compassion during times of crisis.

The compassionate, loving nature of humans has helped humanity to survive countless catastrophes throughout its evolutionary history.

Research indicates that every time humanity faces a natural or self-generated disaster, there is a surge in compassion and altruism.

When humans risk their own life to save that of another, compassion is expressed through heroic acts of courage and selflessness.

What is a simple way to show compassion?

Be kind.

Navigate life with kindness

Smiling at others or saying please, thank you, and have a nice day are all simple acts of kindness to share with other humans in day-to-day life.

Create opportunities for kindness.

Be present in the company of others.

When humans stare down at their phones, they miss out on opportunities to connect with others and share kindness.

Feel the effects of kindness.

Being kind to others activates the human brain's reward system as if the giver was the recipient of the act of kindness.

Kindness always comes back in return.

Whenever a human is kind to others, they are kind to themselves. That's because kindness is reciprocal. It's the gift that gives back.

What are the physics of compassion and kindness?

The law of reflection.

Direct light reflects off an object and bounces back to the source of light and in new directions.

SUBATOMIC LIGHT	HUMAN LIGHT
When electrons release energy, they give off light.	When humans are kind to others, they give off light.

The law of human kindness.

The light of human kindness bounces back to the giver of the kind act, and amazingly, it even touches others who witnessed the act of kindness.

When humans make an effort to be kind to someone without seeking anything in return their true self shines bright.

Self-Reflection

Compassion.

Compassion requires looking beyond one's suffering to help alleviate the pain of other humans in need.

How often do I put others before myself? Why?

How do I feel when I help others in need? Why?

Who in life needs more of my compassion? Why?

What suffering and hardships have they endured?

Am I educated on what they have gone through?

In what ways can I get involved to help out?

What is the **fourth step** to loving unconditionally?

Be forgiving.

Forgiveness is the letting go of thoughts such as anger, hatred, resentment, and revenge.

Forgiveness does not condone acts of dishonesty, abuse, or violence toward other humans.

The most difficult person for a human to forgive is themselves because the unconscious mind is notorious for holding on to regrets from the past.

The biology of anger.

Anger activates the human stress response, which often leads to depression, illness, and disease.

The benefits of forgiveness.

Less stress leads to healthier relationships and also improves physical and mental well-being.

"Holding on to anger is like grasping a hot coal with the intent of throwing it at someone else; you are the one who gets burned."
-Buddha

How do humans practice forgiveness?

Empathy & compassion.

Letting go of the hot coals of anger, hatred, and resentment through empathy and compassion is essential for humans to experience unconditional love.

The choice to forgive is the choice to help one's self.

Forgiveness begins at home.

About eighty percent of humans grow up in dysfunctional homes, which underscores the importance of practicing forgiveness.

Forgiveness tips.

Accept each other's unique traits.

Listen to each other's point of view.

Avoid character attacks.

Resolve conflicts peacefully.

Don't go to bed, angry or upset.

Love unconditionally.

Humans don't have to like or approve of how others wronged them, but they do have to accept the reality of the situation, forgive, move on, and find peace.

Why does the unconscious mind resist forgiveness?

The unconscious mind is self-righteous.

The unconscious mind falsely believes its thoughts, beliefs, and actions must always be right, while opposing viewpoints must always be wrong.

Symptoms of self-righteousness.

Constantly judging.

No empathy, compassion, or forgiveness for the ignorance and mistakes of others.

Never admitting or apologizing when proven wrong, even when there is proof of a mistake.

Using generosity for the sole purpose of elevating oneself above others.

Refusing to listen to others' thoughts, opinions, or ideas.

Self-righteous humans are unconsciously blinded by the false belief that anger, character attacks, and sometimes even violence are justified when others don't share their beliefs.

Self-Reflection

Forgiveness.

Forgiveness often brings more peace to the forgiver than those that needed forgiveness.

Is it easy or difficult for me to forgive? How come?

Have I ever needed forgiveness from others? Why?

When was the last time I forgave someone? Why?

How did it feel to move past what happened?

Is there anyone I currently need to forgive? Why?

How would I benefit from letting go of the past?

What are the steps to love unconditionally?

1. LOVE YOURSELF
Nourish the mind, body, and spirit.

2. DISPLAY EMPATHY
Be aware of other humans' feelings.

3. HAVE COMPASSION
Help to relieve the suffering of others.

4. BE FORGIVING
Let go of anger, hate, and revenge.

Example

Event: "That car just cut me off."

Empathy: "The driver must have been distracted."

Compassion: "I've also been distracted while driving."

Forgiveness: "No problem...it is what it is."

Why is romantic love between humans in crisis?

Romantic love is becoming conditional.

Many humans create a list or set of criteria to find their ideal partner; this often leads to unrealistic expectations and places certain conditions on love.

Social media addiction unconsciously promotes conditional love through self-obsession and the constant judgment of other humans.

SMART PHONES	SOCIAL MEDIA
Cell phones reduce face to face interactions needed for romantic relationships.	Posting leads to narcissism, which hinders one's ability to express empathy and connect with others.
Monitoring alerts, texts, and email messages create chronic stress, which inhibits the human sex drive.	Making comparisons leads to jealousy and also reduces romatic desires.

The human addiction to technology has put the future of romantic partnerships in jeopardy.

What is required for loving relationships?

Acceptance.

Every human has unique genes, life experiences, and personality traits; when their partner does not accept these fixed traits, a lifetime of conflict often follows.

Communication.

Loving partnership requires open communication and the expression of empathy, compassion, kindness, and forgiveness.

Trust.

Trust is the instinctive human need for safety and security. Without it, no human relationship can endure the test of time.

Psychologist and researcher John Gottman predicted with over 90 percent accuracy if a couple would get divorced by observing four negative behaviors.

1. Criticism - attacking one's character.

2. Contempt - condescending and hurtful words.

3. Defensiveness - being in denial of a hurtful act.

4. Stonewalling – withdrawing from communication.

Romantic love flourishes when partners accept each other for who they are, not who they want them to be.

THE FORMULA TO KNOW YOUR TRUE SELF

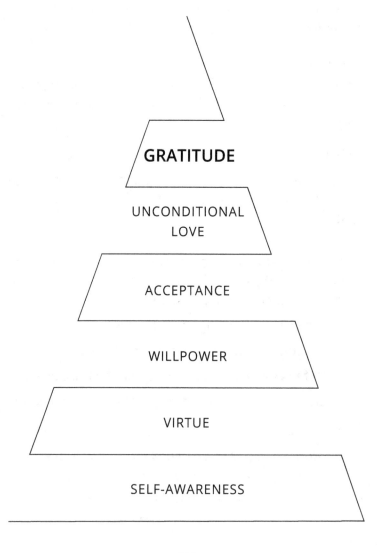

GRATITUDE

UNCONDITIONAL LOVE

ACCEPTANCE

WILLPOWER

VIRTUE

SELF-AWARENESS

What is gratitude?

To give thanks.

Gratitude is the peace and joy a human feels when one takes the time to appreciate the gifts and experiences in the present moment.

Being grateful for what is and the gifts one has brings peace to the unconscious mind.

The benefits of gratitude.

Gratitude helps humans stay in the moment.

Generates enthusiasm and love for life.

It helps humans overcome any catastrophic loss.

Decreases envy, resentment, and greed.

Reduces anxiety and depression.

Strengthens the immune system.

Diminishes worry about the future.

Countless gifts go unappreciated by humans every moment.

Why is expressing gratitude under-appreciated?

Humans take life's gifts for granted.

The unconscious mind does not appreciate the gifts found in life until they are lost.

Living in a materialistic world full of wants and desires blinds humans to the gifts they already have.

THE POWER IS ON	THE POWER IS OUT
Many humans seldom appreciate the gift of electricity every time they turn on a light switch.	Humans always appreciate electricity when they lose power and have to live in darkness.

Innovations have become so commonplace that they have become expected and not appreciated by many humans.

What fuels ingratitude among humans?

Getting lost in the feed.

Many humans stay tethered to their phones 24/7, triggering wants and desires in their unconscious minds through an endless stream of content that fuels ingratitude.

SOCIAL MEDIA	ADVERTISING

Comparisons, jealousy, and obsessions with creating content to earn "likes" all take humans out of the present moment where gratitude exists.	A stream of targeted advertisements creates desire and usually makes humans feel like their life is deficient in one way or another.

Humans must learn to put the phone down and not make it their reality because this addiction leads to anxiety and depression.

How do humans practice gratitude?

Reflect, embrace, and direct.

Reflect on human existence.

While humans may live in a materialistic world full of wants and desires, they can always reflect on and appreciate the true, spiritual nature of existence.

Embrace all life experiences.

Accepting the reality of all life's experiences, both pleasant and unpleasant, is the seed from which gratitude germinates.

Direct one's consciousness.

When humans direct their consciousness to the present moment, they soon discover a world of gifts around and within them.

When humans embrace their life's experiences and direct their consciousness to the gifts found in the present moment, they experience their true self.

What is the ultimate source of gratitude?

Universal Intelligence.

Universal intelligence manifests itself through the gifts found in nature and the human experience.

NATURE	HUMAN EXPERIENCE
Human existence on planet earth.	To observe and direct one's thoughts.
The endless inspiration found in nature.	To experience the various human senses.
The air we breathe and the water we drink.	To partner in creation and share passions.
The plants and animals that sustain human life.	To experience and share unconditional love.
The resources humans use for innovation.	To connect with family, friends, and community.

Every human has something to be grateful for.

How do humans express gratitude for nature?

Preserving and enjoying its beauty.

There are hundreds-of-thousands of organizations devoted to preserving nature and living creatures, such as The National Audobon Society, the Wildlife Conservation Society, and Oceana.

Billions of humans show their love and appreciation for nature by visiting the earth's oceans, lakes, mountains, rivers, streams, parks, and wildlife preserves.

ENVIRONMENTAL IGNORANCE	STEWARDS OF THE EARTH
Humanity's ignorance and denial of how deeply interconnected we are with nature have severely damaged the earth's diverse ecosystem.	Expressing gratitude for nature also comes with a commitment for every human to take an active role in its protection and conservation.

Raising human consciousness will help eliminate ignorance and sustain the environment.

When can humans easily express gratitude?

Anytime.

When gratitude becomes a daily practice, it rewires the unconscious mind to appreciate more and complain less.

The Morning.

When humans express gratitude upon waking, it centers them in their true self for a blissful start to the day.

Mealtime.

Food is both a life-sustaining and highly sensory experience that can always be appreciated.

At Night.

Gratitude before bed quiets thoughts from the unconscious mind and relaxes the body for restful sleep.

Gratitude is the daily ritual of wise humans.

Self-Reflection

Gratitude.

When the expression of gratitude becomes a daily habit, humans find new meaning and joy in life.

Do I take anything in life for granted? How come?

When was the last time I expressed gratitude? Why?

Who am I grateful to have as part of my life? Why?

What life experiences am I grateful for? Why?

How does It feel when I express gratitude? Why?

Will I make expressing gratitude a daily habit? How?

How does gratitude help humans navigate life's uncertainty?

Keeping humans centered.

Expressing gratitude during both pleasant and unpleasant times helps keep humans centered in the true self while navigating through life's experiences.

DURING PLEASANT EVENTS	DURING UNPLEASANT EVENTS
Expressing gratitude during pleasant events helps humans savor the joy found in the experience.	Expressing gratitude during unpleasant life experiences helps to minimize human pain and suffering.

There is a gift in every experience, both pleasant and unpleasant — expressing gratitude helps to identify that gift.

THE FORMULA TO KNOW YOUR TRUE SELF

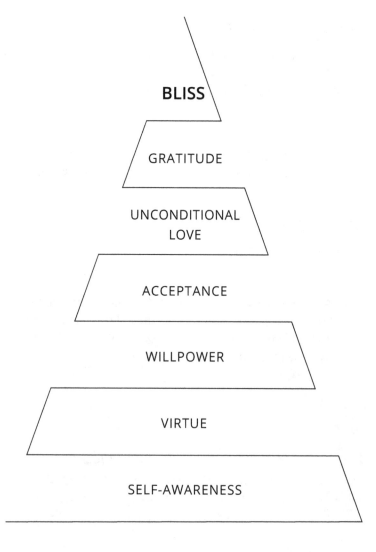

BLISS

GRATITUDE

UNCONDITIONAL
LOVE

ACCEPTANCE

WILLPOWER

VIRTUE

SELF-AWARENESS

How does the unconscious mind seek bliss?

Wants and desires.

FAME

VANITY

OBJECTS

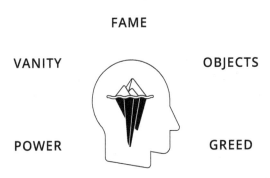

POWER

GREED

The unconscious mind is filled with the false belief that having more things in the material world will lead to greater happiness in life.

While living and acting through their true self, humans experience a lasting, blissful state which no material want or desire can compare.

Bliss is independent of the unconscious mind's wants and desires.

What are the physics of bliss?

Energy waves.

Energy waves are invisible, passing through space, matter, and all living things in the universal energy field.

DESTRUCTIVE ENERGY WAVES	CONSTRUCTIVE ENERGY WAVES
↓ ⋀⋀⋀⋀ = ⟋⎯⟋ ↑ ⋁⋁⋁⋁	↑ ⋁⋁⋁⋁ = ⋁⋁⋁ ↑ ⋁⋁⋁⋁
Destructive waves collide with each other.	Constructive waves overlap each other.
Energy is lost.	*Energy compounds.*

How humans choose to channel their energy directly affects their well-being.

How do human thoughts affect bliss?

Thoughts are energy.
Every thought a human has broadcasts energy waves that are either destructive or constructive.

Energy waves attract like frequencies.
The thoughts humans put out into the universe directly impact the world around and within them.

DESTRUCTIVE THOUGHTS CAUSE SUFFERING	CONSTRUCTIVE THOUGHTS CAUSE BLISS
Fear	Empathy
Anger	Compassion
Jealousy	Kindness
Resentment	Gratefulness
Hatred	Forgiveness
Revenge	Unconditional Love

"Your beliefs become your thoughts, your thoughts become your words, your words become your actions, your habits become your values, your values become your destiny."
-Mahatma Gandhi

How do humans overcome destructive thoughts?

Let them go.

Holding onto destructive thought frequencies like fear, worry, and anger throws the human energy system out of balance.

To help let go of troubling thoughts, initiate the relaxation response and redirect one's consciousness to sources of gratitude, love and support.

An unstable atom decays and gives off radiation; an unbalanced human decays through illness and disease.

Self-Reflection

Blissful thinking.

Living in a materialistic world creates a false sense of reality about how humans can experience bliss.

Do I seek happiness in material items? Why?

How is happiness from material objects fleeting?

How do my thoughts impact my joy and contentment?

Do I share constructive thought frequencies? How?

Do I hold onto destructive thought frequencies? Why?

How will I benefit from letting go of destructive thoughts?

How do humans find bliss on earth?

Talent Development.

Human talent is a natural ability or a unique skill for each human to develop, nurture, and fulfill.

Although various human talents may receive different financial compensations, no one human skill is more important or better than another.

Share talents with humanity.

Humans experience bliss when they utilize and share their talents irrespective of the recognition or compensation they receive.

It is through the diversity of talents that the human species has been able to survive and flourish.

Human talents evolve and change throughout one's life; therefore, embracing and accepting change is a fundamental requirement for humans to maintain a state of bliss.

What is the purpose of human talent?

To create.

Human talents are the conduit used by a Universal Intelligence to manifest new creations and innovations.

Every living organism on planet earth has a purpose or talents that align with the whole of creation.

Find meaning and purpose in talent.

Two stonecutters were laying bricks when a passerby asked what they were doing.

One answered,

"I'm laying bricks."

The other replied,

"I'm building a cathedral."

It's not how much talent a human has that determines achievement, but rather the effort or work they put into fulfilling their purpose.

"Meaningful work is not work that is exciting and challenging every moment; it may, rather, be work that is part of a larger endeavor that is infused with meaning."
-Willis Harman

Self-Reflection

Talents.

Every human has innate abilities bestowed upon them that are designed to be nurtured and shared.

What are some of my natural talents and abilities?

How have my talents evolved or changed over time?

What are some specific talents I really excel at?

How do these talents bring me joy and fulfillment?

How do I use my talents to help humanity?

What can I do to further develop my talents?

What action empowers humans to create and innovate?

Goal setting.

Goal setting empowers humans by directing their consciousness to the betterment of one's self and humanity.

FEW DO IT

Only about 3 percent of humans take the time to write down their goals, even though countless research studies confirm the benefits.

BUT IT WORKS

Research indicates that humans who routinely set goals are healthier, happier, and more productive than those that do not set goals.

Why don't more people set goals?

Most humans don't set goals because they have never been educated on the importance of goal setting or are fearful of failing to achieve their desired results.

Without goals, human purpose lacks focus and direction.

What are the guidelines for goal setting?

1. **The goals you choose to establish must be your own.**

2. Set realistic goals based on your unique talents.

3. Write down your goals to create a daily reminder of your intentions.

4. Make sure that your goals are both specific and measurable

5. Identify any additional knowledge you might need to attain your goals.

6. Identify individuals who would be willing to support you on your journey.

7. Identify any potential roadblocks you may experience moving forward.

8. Establish short and long-term goals with specific time frames and success measurements.

9. Visualize the attainment of your goal upon waking and before sleep.

10. Manage your time with a daily to-do list and act on your plan.

How does goal setting promote bliss?

Goals help bring balance to one's life.

Identify where you would rate yourself today in each goal category by placing a dot at the 0, 25%, 50%, 75%, or 100% mark.

Connect the dots to determine what aspects of your life require more focus and attention.

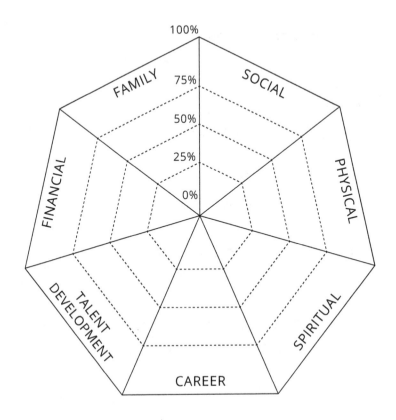

What is an example of a properly set goal?

Example goal.
Spend less screen time on my phone.

How will I benefit?
I'll have more time to enjoy the present moment, and I'll spend less time comparing myself to others.

What do I need to know?
My current daily average screen time.

My support resources:
Family, friends, and work colleagues.

Potential roadblocks:
Habits and feeling disconnected.

Time frame for achievement:
A daily analysis of screen time.

Success measurement:
10 percent reduction in phone screen time.

How are goals put into an action plan?

Daily to-do lists.

Example:

Spend less screen time on my phone.

☐ Keep my phone off until after breakfast.

☐ Turn off my phone when I am eating with others.

☐ Ask those I'm with to turn off their phones during meals.

☐ Meditate when I get an urge to check my social feeds.

☐ Leave my phone at home when outside enjoying nature.

☐ Set my phone on airplane mode before I go to bed.

To-do lists focus human consciousness on the achievement of one's goals while staying centered in the true self.

What process helps humans manifest their goals?

The visualization process.

Step 1:
Determine what you want.

Begin the visualization process by reviewing your goals and determining how you and others would benefit from achieving them.

Step 2:
Maintain a relaxed state.

Visualizing the desired outcome of the goal during meditative practices connects humans with the vibrational frequency of Universal Intelligence, the source of creation.

Step 3:
Visualize every detail.

Humans manifest goals faster and more successfully when they regularly visualize the attainment of their ambitions in vivid detail through the power of imagination.

Every human has an imagination, but many humans never learn how to leverage their imagination to attain their goals.

How do humans create and innovate together?

Collaboration.

Cooperative alliances have fueled all of humanity's achievements from primitive tribes to modern society.

The physics of collaboration.

When energy waves move in the same direction, the combined energy wave has a higher amplitude than the amplitude of any of the individual energy waves combined to produce it.

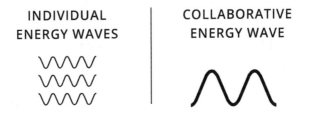

INDIVIDUAL ENERGY WAVES	COLLABORATIVE ENERGY WAVE

Collective human consciousness.

Coherence is the state when energy waves created by collective human consciousness match those of Universal Intelligence. When in a state of coherence, teams operate as "one" consciousness.

"If you want to find the secrets of the universe, think in terms of energy, frequency, and vibration."
-Nikola Tesla

What is crucial for effective collaboration?

Contribute through the true self.

Harnessing the power of collective human consciousness is only possible when groups, teams, and organizations can eliminate the destructive thought frequencies of anger, hatred, jealousy, and self-righteousness.

DON'T BLAME	SHARE SUCCESS

Consciously connected teams don't blame others for setbacks when working on shared goals but rather see challenges as opportunities to learn and grow as one.	Conscious contributors believe in recognizing others for achievements because no one individual is as smart as the collective consciousness of the team.

High-performance teams work together in a spirit of harmony, trust, and mutual respect.

Self-Reflection

Manifesting creation.

When humans partner with Universal Intelligence and each other, they can create new realities.

What goals do I currently have set for my life? Why?

In what aspects of my life can I set new goals? Why?

Do I visualize my goals becoming a reality? How?

How does visualization help manifest goals?

How can collaboration help to achieve my vision?

How can I improve how I collaborate with others?

What keeps humans grounded when they achieve goals?

Humility.

Humility places low importance on the unconscious mind's needs, such as fame, greed, and power.

Humility places high importance on giving recognition to other humans and a higher power for achievements.

The gifts of humility.

Humility helps humans remain open to personal growth and development opportunities.

Humility is a well-known and respected quality of leaders in all aspects of human life.

Staying humble keeps humans grounded in their true self while living in a materialistic world.

"Those in whom we recognize genius commonly disclaim it. A universal characteristic of genius is humility. The genius has always attributed his insights to some higher influence."
- David R. Hawkins

What achievements are humans ultimately remembered for?

Achievements of the true self.

When the mortal self dies, family and friends celebrate the spiritual dimensions of the deceased.

Examples from actual obituaries, names have been removed.

LOVE

Married for 70 years, they held hands at breakfast every morning, and died just 15 hours apart.

KINDNESS

She spent her life as a kind, gentle soul, always helped others, and asked for nothing in return.

CONNECTEDNESS

An amazing steward of the earth and a profound lover of nature who lived her life with an open heart.

ACCEPTANCE

Wheelchair-bound for life with quadriplegia, he viewed himself as very fortunate in life.

Human achievement lies not in what we can get from the world but rather in what we can give.

What clues exist about the true self after death?

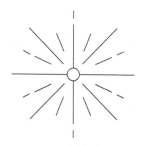

The laws of nature.

Consciousness = Light.

Light = Energy.

Energy never dies.

All energy connects to one source, Universal Intelligence.

Near death experiences (NDE).

Dr. Bruce Greyson analyzed over 1,000 cases of near-death experience and discovered that it's possible for consciousness to function outside the human body.

Reincarnation research.

Dr. Jim Tucker studied 2,500 cases since 1960, and his research indicates that reincarnation is real and consciousness remains after the body dies.

Most of us fear death on some level, but humans report an overwhelming sense of peace, unconditional love, and bliss in near-death experiences.

Self-Reflection

Remembrance.

After mortal death, humans are most often remembered by how they acted through their true selves.

How do I want to be remembered by others?

What would they write about my life? Why?

How will my existence have helped humanity?

What causes will I have helped to support?

What will be my most significant achievements?

What lasting impression will I make on the world?

Raising human consciousness

How are humans responsible for their own evolution?

Choice.

Humans differentiate themselves from other animals by having the unique ability to choose how they respond to life's experiences.

Mind/spirit duality.

A human can choose to unconsciously respond to life's events through their mind or consciously through their true self.

Example:
Have you ever seen a human hate and love at the same time?

The choice of consciousness.

The choice of consciousness over unconsciousness provides humans with the opportunity to take an active role in their evolution to flourish and grow, regardless of life's circumstances.

"Everything can be taken from a man but one thing: the last of human freedoms — to choose one's attitude in any given set of circumstances, to choose one's own way."
- Dr Viktor Frankl

What are wise choices to raise human consciousness?

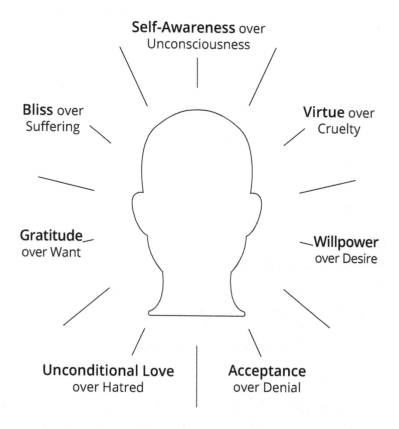

Self-Awareness over Unconsciousness

Bliss over Suffering

Virtue over Cruelty

Gratitude over Want

Willpower over Desire

Unconditional Love over Hatred

Acceptance over Denial

Are making wise choices easy for humans?

No.

Instincts.
Identifying and acting through the true self is not instinctive for most humans and must be learned.

The mind.
Humans must remain vigilant to overcome the negative thoughts, emotions, and desires that regularly surface from the unconscious mind.

The body.
Illness, disease, lack of sleep, and poor nutrition all throw the human energy system out of balance, making wise decisions difficult.

The media.
The news, advertising, and social media fuel the desires and fears of the unconscious mind.

Personal commitment.
Knowing the true self is not a 30, 60, or 90-day challenge; it's a moment-to-moment lifetime commitment.

What is the key choice in raising human consciousness?

To live through the true self.

Human life is a chaotic, complex system with underlying laws and formulas that correlate with peace, joy, and contentment.

When humans practice actions in the formula to know your true self, their energy vibrates at the same frequency of nature and Universal Intelligence.

Identifying with and act through the true self is the most generous contribution humans can make for themselves and humanity.

What is the formula to know your true self?

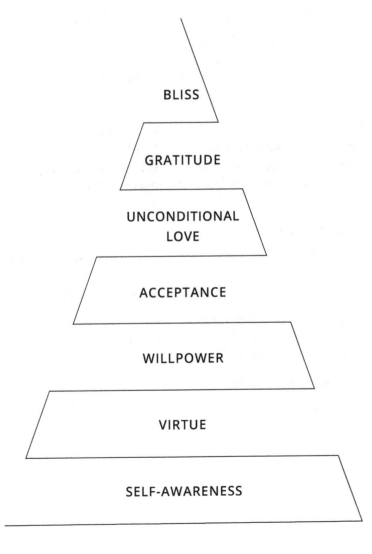

BLISS

GRATITUDE

UNCONDITIONAL
LOVE

ACCEPTANCE

WILLPOWER

VIRTUE

SELF-AWARENESS

How can we raise the consciousness of humanity?

One human at a time.

The next evolution of humanity will require the transformation of unconscious humans into highly conscious ones.

Schools, institutions, and spiritual teachings can only support humans on their journey to knowing their true selves; everyone is responsible for practicing actions to raise their level of consciousness.

It starts with you.

On the journey to knowing your true self, you have to look inward and become your own teacher and advocate. You have to learn to help yourself.

Change comes from within and requires a commitment to personal growth. There are no shortcuts to discovering your true self.

Enjoy the journey.

Appendix

Valued Resources

A New Earth by Eckhart Tolle

Be As You Are by David Godman

Being Aware of Being Aware by Rupert Spira

Being Mortal by Atul Gawande

Born for Love by Bruce Perry

Buddha's Brain by Rick Hanson and Richard Mendius

Character Strengths and Virtues by Christopher Peterson and Martin Seligman

Creativity by Mihaly Csikszentmihalyi

Emotional Intelligence by Daniel Goleman

Evidence of the Afterlife by Jerry Long

Flourish by Martin E. P. Seligman

Full Catastrophe Living by Jon Kabat-Zinn

Flow by Mihaly Csikszentmihalyi

From Science to God by Peter Russell

How to Stop Worrying and Start Living by Dale Carnagie

Imagine Heaven by John Burke

Man's Search for Meaning by Viktor Frankl

On Grief and Grieving by Elisabeth Kübler-Ross

Valued Resources

Power Through Constuctive Thinking by Emmet Fox

Power vs. Force by David R. Hawkins

Proof of Heaven by Eben Alexander

Sapiens: A Brief History of Humankind by Yuval Noah Harari

Seat of the Soul by Gary Zukav

Seeking the Heart of Wisdom by Joseph Goldstein and Jack Kornfield

Stumbling on Happiness by Daniel Gilbert

Swedenborg by Gary Lachman

Tao Te Ching by Lao Tze

Thanks! by Robert Emmons

The Analects by Confucius

The Art of Living by Sharon Lebell

The Biology of Belief by Bruce Lipton

The Brain Book by Peter Russell

The Brain by David Eagleman

The Brain that Changes Itself by Norman Doidge

The Essential Writings of Emerson by Ralph Waldo Emerson

The Field by Lynne McTaggart

Valued Resources

The Future of the Mind by Micho Kaku

The Hero with a Thousand Faces by Joseph Campbell

The Holographic Universe by Michael Talbot

The How of Happiness by Sonja Lyubomirsky

The Invisible Gorilla by Christopher Chabris

The Power of Habit by Charles Duhigg

The Shallows by Nicholas Carr

Gandhi: An Autobiography - The Story of My Experiments With Truth by Mohandas K. Gandhi

The Undiscovered Self by C.G. Jung

The Untethered Soul by Michael Singer

The Upanishads by Alistair Shearer and Peter Russell

The Willpower Instinct by Kelly McGonigal

The World According to Physics by Jim Al-Khalili

There is a River by Thomas Sugrue

Willpower by Roy F. Baumeister and John Tierney

About the author

James Petrossi is an advocate for humanity and the founder of PTNL, which helps organizations, leaders, and students realize their potential by raising their consciousness.

He utilizes experience in talent development, creative strategy, and decades of research into the human condition to offer practical solutions that help transform people's lives.

James graduated from Fairfield University with a degree in organizational communications and psychology. He currently lives in Austin, Texas with his wife Samantha and devotes his time to writing, speaking, and helping others.

Visit ptnl.com for additional resources.

Have the concepts presented in *Know Your True Self* helped you in some way? If so, I would love to hear about it. Posting honest reviews online is helpful for both authors and potential readers.

Thank You.

- James Petrossi